Looking at Life Cycles

Cat

Victoria Huseby

A⁺

Smart Apple Media

Smart Apple Media is published by Black Rabbit Books
P.O. Box 3263, Mankato, Minnesota 56002

Printed in the United States

Published by arrangement with the Watts Publishing Group Ltd, London.

Editor: Rachel Tonkin
Designer: Chris Fraser
Picture researcher: Diana Morris
Science consultant: Andrew Solway
Literacy consultant: Gill Matthews
Illustrations: John Alston

Picture credits:
Raymond Blythe/OSF: 9; Jane Burton/Nature PL: 11; Corbis: 5;
DK Ltd/Corbis: 7; Angela Hampton/RSPCA PL; front cover, 13.
Mitsuaki Iwago/Minden Pictures/FLPA Images: 19; Jane Knight/NHPA: 15;
LBC Images/Alamy: 1, 21; Zoomteam/Shutterstock: 17.

Library of Congress Cataloging-in-Publication Data

Huseby, Victoria.
    Cat / by Victoria Huseby.
    p. cm.—(Smart Apple Media. Looking at life cycles)
    Summary: "An introduction to the life cycle of a cat, including pregnancy,
giving birth, growing up, and becoming an adult"—Provided by publisher.
    Includes index.
    ISBN 978-1-59920-177-1
    1. Cats—Life cycles—Juvenile literature. I. Title.
SF445.7.H87 2009
636.8—dc22
                                                                          2007030464

9 8 7 6 5 4 3 2 1

Contents

Pregnancy 4

Giving Birth 6

Feeding 8

Hearing and Seeing 10

Walking 12

Solid Food 14

Playing 16

Washing 18

Adulthood 20

Cat Facts and Glossary 22

Index and Web Sites 24

Pregnancy

When a female cat is **pregnant**, baby cats grow inside her. A baby cat is called a **kitten**.

Giving Birth

A cat can give birth to as many as 10 kittens in one **litter**. The mother cat licks the newborn kittens. This cleans the kittens and helps wake them up.

Feeding

The mother cat feeds the kittens with her **milk.** This is all the kittens eat for six weeks.

9

Hearing and Seeing

Kittens cannot see or hear when they are born. They begin to hear when they are about 12 days old. Their eyes stay closed for about 14 days.

Walking

Kittens learn to walk
when they are about 17
days old. Until then,
they fall over a lot!

Solid Food

Kittens begin to eat **solid food** when they are about six weeks old. They can eat moist or dry cat food.

15

Playing

Kittens and cats love to play. Playing helps kittens grow stronger. It also teaches them **hunting skills**. Kittens like to play with balls and other toys.

Washing

Kittens lick themselves to keep clean. Their rough tongues help remove any dirt. They use their **paws** to wash behind their ears.

Adulthood

Most cats are fully grown
by the time they are seven
months old. At this age,
a female cat can have
kittens of her own.

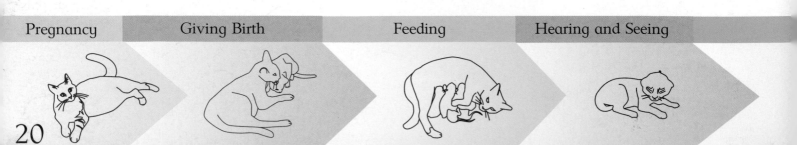

Pregnancy   Giving Birth   Feeding   Hearing and Seeing

Walking   Solid Food   Playing   Adulthood

Cat Facts

- A cat's sense of smell is 14 times stronger than a human's.

- A cat uses its tail to help keep its balance.

- A cat uses its whiskers to feel whether it can fit into a small space. Cats' whiskers are sensitive to touch.

- Cats will usually have between 2 and 6 kittens at one time, but they can have up to 10 in a litter.

- On average, a cat will sleep for 16 hours a day.

- Cats normally have five toes on their front paws and four toes on their back paws.

- Cats can live for 16 years or more.

Glossary

Hunting skills
The ability to catch and kill animals for food.

Kitten
A baby cat is called a kitten.

Litter
A group of animals born at the same time to one mother.

Milk
The mother cat's body makes special milk that helps the kittens grow.

Paws
Animals' feet. A cat has four paws.

Pregnant
When a female cat has kittens growing inside her.

Solid food
Food that a kitten eats after it is too old for its mother's milk, such as dry or canned cat food.

Index and Web Sites

birth 6

cats 4, 6, 8, 16, 20, 22, 23

feeding 8

hearing 10

hunting skills 16, 23

kittens 4, 6, 8, 10, 12, 14,
     16, 18, 20, 22, 23

litter 6, 22, 23

milk 8, 23

paws 18, 22, 23

playing 16

pregnant 4, 23

seeing 10

solid food 14, 23

tongues 18

walking 12

washing 18

whiskers 22

For Kids:

ASPCA Animaland: The Web Site for Kids who Love Animals!
http://www.aspca.org/site/PageServer?
   pagename=kids_home

American Veterinary Medical Association's Care for Animals Kid's Corner
http://www.avma.org/careforanimals/
   kidscorner

FDA Kids' Site—Cat Care
http://www.fda.gov/oc/opacom/kids/
   html/cat_care.htm

For Teachers:

A to Z Teachers' Stuff: Life Cycles
http://atozteacherstuff.com/Themes/
   Life_Cycles/

ProTeacher! Life Science Lesson Plans
http://www.proteacher.com/110003.shtml